WELCOME TO OUR WORLD

SECOND EDITION

SERIES EDITORS

Joan Kang Shin & JoAnn (Jodi) Crandall

**NATIONAL
GEOGRAPHIC
LEARNING**

Australia • Brazil • Canada • Mexico • Singapore • United Kingdom • United States

Hello!

Listen and circle. Say. TR: AB.0.1

Draw and say.

My name is

_____.

1 Eyes, Nose, Mouth

VOCABULARY Look and say. Find and circle.

SONG Listen and draw. **TR: AB.1.1**

THE SOUNDS OF ENGLISH Listen and say. Circle. **TR: AB.1.2**

  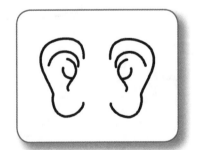 

CONCEPTS Count and draw a line.

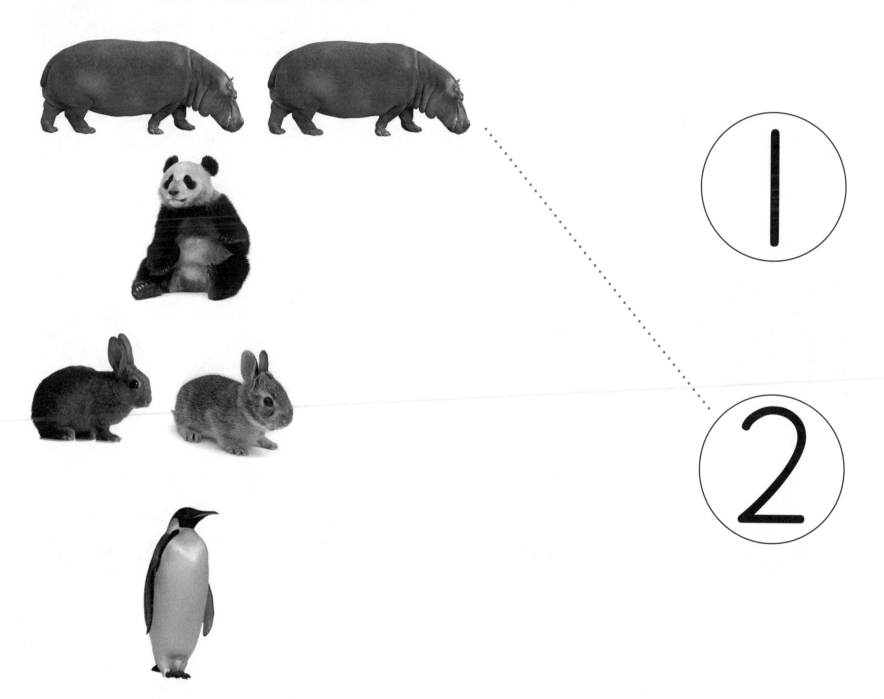

I've got two eyes.

2 My Home

SONG Listen and circle. Colour. TR: AB.2.1

THE SOUNDS OF ENGLISH Listen and say. Circle. TR: AB.2.2

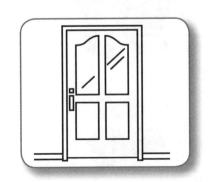   

CONCEPTS Look and circle. Use red for *open*. Use blue for *close*.

LANGUAGE IN USE   Listen. Trace and say. TR: AB.2.3

This is my mummy.

3 Snack Time

SONG Find the bananas. Draw a line. TR: AB.3.1

THE SOUNDS OF ENGLISH Listen and say. Circle. TR: AB.3.2

CONCEPTS Say. Draw and count.

5

4

3

What do you want?

I want a banana, please.

4 My Dress Is Yellow

VOCABULARY   Say and draw a line.

SONG Listen and colour. TR: AB.4.1

THE SOUNDS OF ENGLISH Listen and say. Circle. TR: AB.4.2

CONCEPTS Colour red, yellow or blue. Say.

LANGUAGE IN USE   Listen. Trace and colour. Say. TR: AB.4.3

What colour is your shirt?

It's yellow.

Review

Find and colour. Count and circle.

1 2 3 4 5	1 2 3 4 5	1 2 3 4 5	1 2 3 4 5	1 2 3 4 5

Trace. Colour the clothes blue, red and yellow. Say.

5 Family

VOCABULARY   Draw a line and say.

SONG Listen and draw. TR: AB.5.1

THE SOUNDS OF ENGLISH Listen and say. Circle. TR: AB.5.2

CONCEPTS   Say and draw a line.

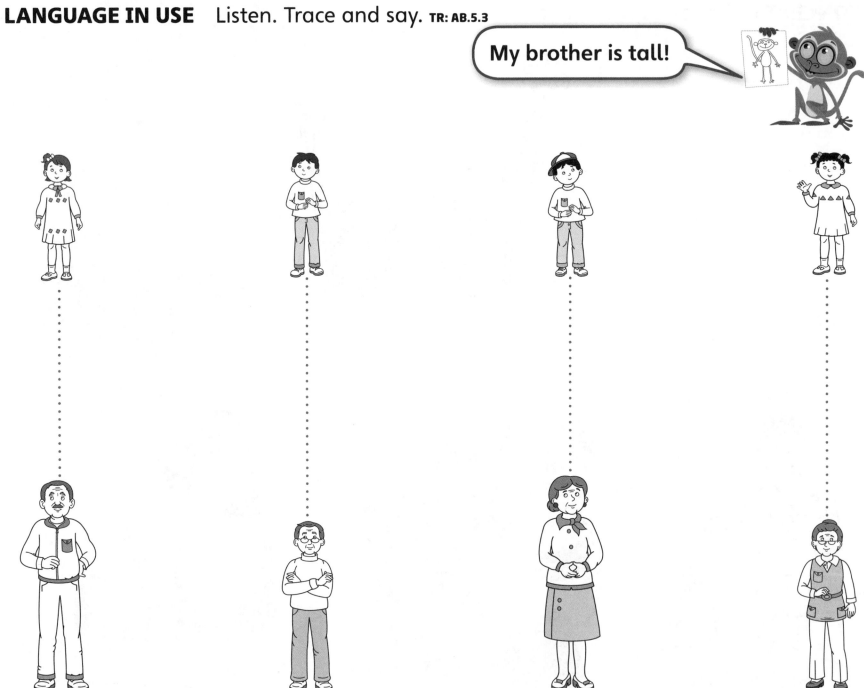

My brother is tall!

6 I Like Trains

VOCABULARY   Listen and say. Circle. TR: AB.6.1

SONG   Listen and colour. TR: AB.6.2

THE SOUNDS OF ENGLISH   Listen and say. Circle. TR: AB.6.3

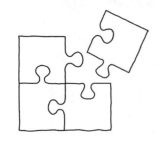    

CONCEPTS Trace and draw a line. Say.

I like trains.

7 My Dog Is Small

VOCABULARY Draw a line. Point and say.

SONG Listen and circle. TR: AB.7.1

THE SOUNDS OF ENGLISH Listen and say. Circle. TR: AB.7.2

CONCEPTS   Look and say. Circle.

8 Look at the Insect!

VOCABULARY Draw a line and say.

SONG   Listen. Choose and circle. Colour. TR: AB.8.1

THE SOUNDS OF ENGLISH   Listen and say. Circle. TR: AB.8.2

CONCEPTS   Colour the picture green, orange, pink and purple. Say.

LANGUAGE IN USE Listen. Trace and draw. Say. TR: AB.8.3

Look at the flower!

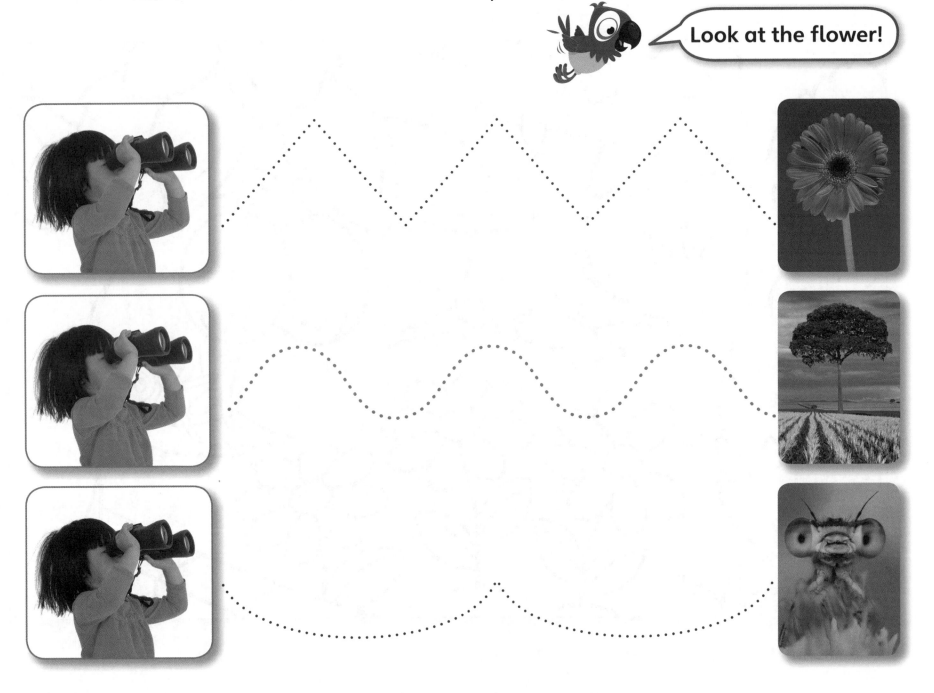

Review

Listen and colour. **TR: AB.8.6**

Find and trace. Say.

Unit 1

Count and say.

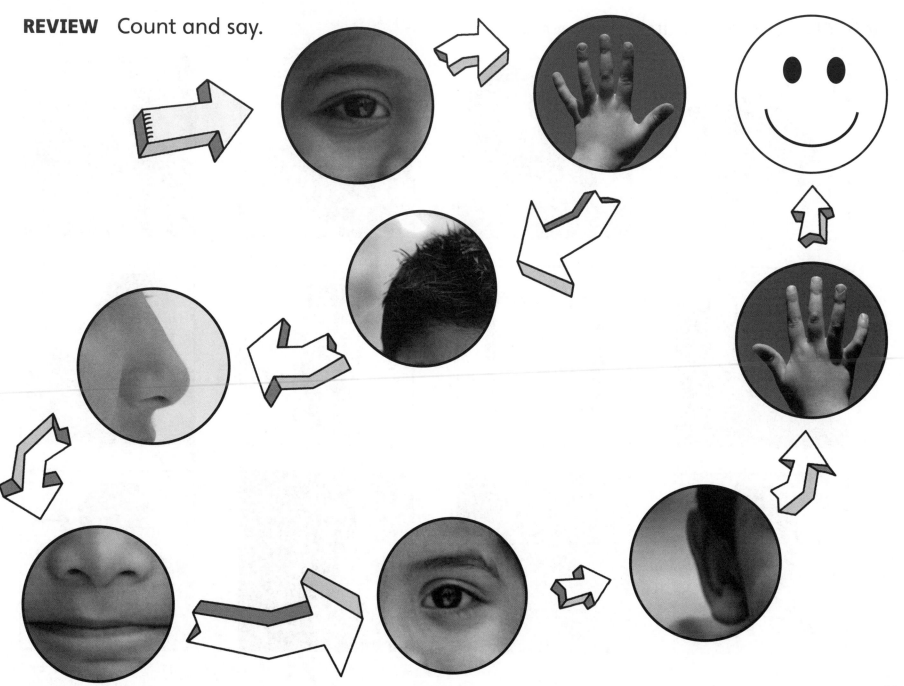

Unit 2

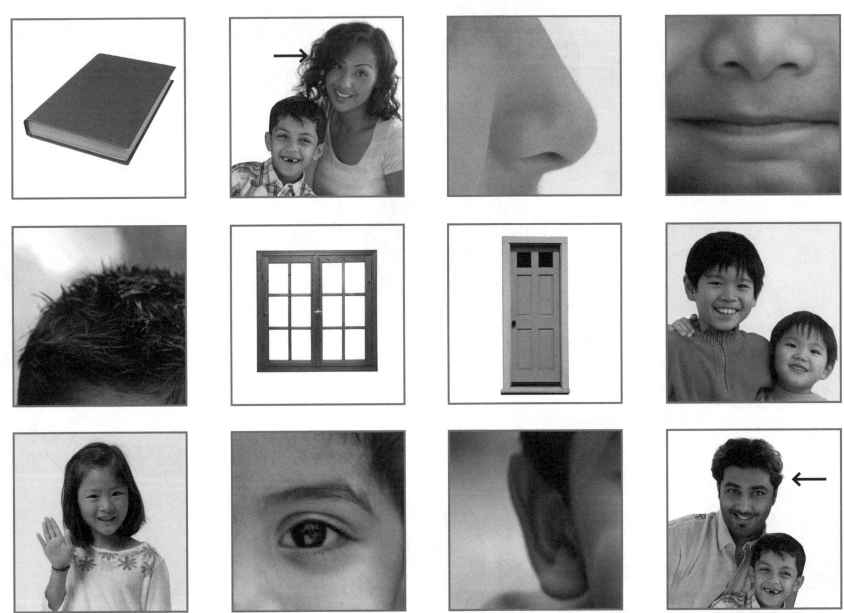

Unit 3

REVIEW Find and count. Colour.

1   2   3   4   5

Unit 4

REVIEW Look and say.

Unit 5

REVIEW Look and draw a line. Say.

Unit 6

REVIEW Count and say.

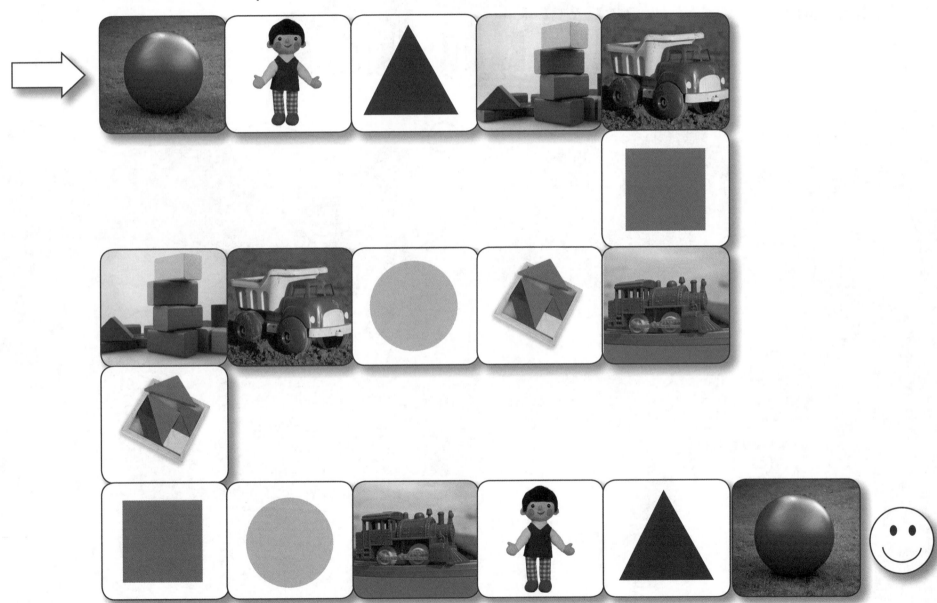

Unit 7

Draw a line and say.

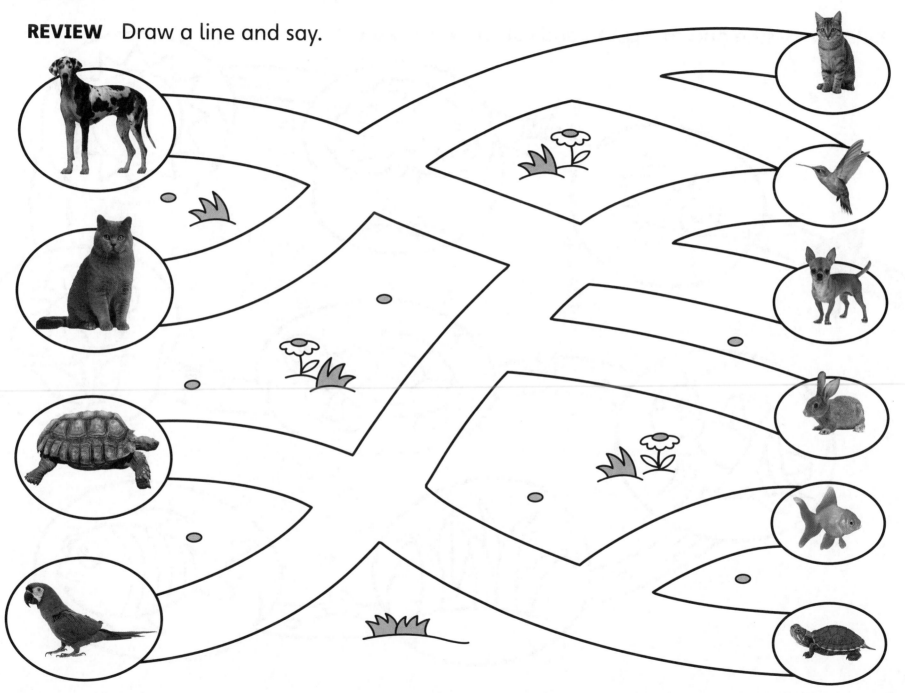

47

Unit 8

REVIEW Listen and say. Listen and colour. **TR: AB.8.4, AB.8.5**

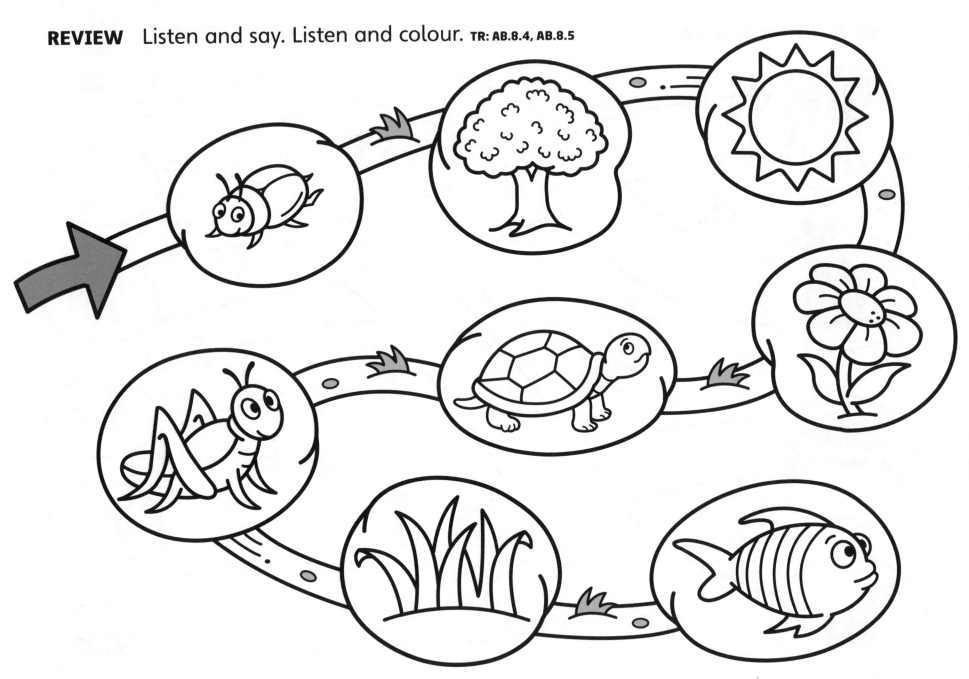